Shorten your Job Search

Less stress, More money

Introduction

Are you trying to find a new job, but not sure of the best way to pursue a new position? You are not alone. The path to a new job can be rocky, filled with turns, delays and unexpected bumps. This book was designed by a long-time staffing industry expert to help you organize your search, shorten the length of time to finding a new job, provide insight into the hiring process, and teach you how to maximize your earnings potential. You will find tips that will make you stand out from other applicants and provide you with an insider's edge into landing the job that you want and in advancing your career. The information outlined in this book is designed to make your job search shorter, easier, more organized, and less stressful.

Foreword

The average job search takes over six weeks. However, that number can be considerably longer depending on the industry, your experience, and the level of position that you seek. The age of the job hunter and a higher desired salary can oftentimes lead to searches of four months or longer. If you factor in things such as an uncertain economy, the timeframe can look downright depressing.

On average, recruiters spend just *six seconds* looking at a résumé before deciding whether or not a person is a potential fit for their position. Think about that – six seconds decide whether or not your résumé makes it into the "reject pile", the "maybe pile", or the "must interview pile". Six seconds. Is that fair to you? No, but it is the reality, which means you need to have a background that jumps off the page.

Table of Contents

- Questions – What to Ask, What not to Ask
- What to Take to the interview
- Group Interviews
- Post Interview/Follow up tips – Notes, Emails, and Phone Calls
- How Much Contact is Too Much? When to Let Go and Cut Your Losses?
- What If You Are Not Offered A Position?

Chapter Seven: I received an offer, now what?
(Page 45)

- Compensation and Negotiating
- Counter Offers
- In Conclusion

Chapter One

The Résumé

Résumé Basics:

A well thought out and carefully written résumé is a door opener. It is a marketing piece. And it is a living history document that spells out who you are, for whom you have worked, where you have worked, what you have done, how you performed those duties, and why a potential employer should talk to you.

The objective of every résumé is to stir interest and create desire in an employer. It should make them want to sit down with you in person to discuss how you can help them solve whatever problem, bottleneck, or objective they may have. A well-written résumé serves as a vehicle to create interest and showcase your abilities to an employer. The résumé creates the opportunity to sell yourself in person, and discuss what you have done in the past, and what you can do to help an employer in the future.

Details such as current and prior employer information, dates of employment, duties, and major accomplishments are items you will need to include. It is important to be concise and provide quantifiable information that will be pertinent as to what an employer will want to see such as revenue generated, budgets managed, and the number and types of employees managed are things that may be appropriate and considered "standard" for many positions. Using your personal insight and perspective on your field should give you some guidance as to what you should include on your résumé and will be pertinent to helping you land your next job.

Your résumé should demonstrate your success as it relates to the position description and in context to the hiring manager's needs and objectives. Having multiple versions of your résumé suitable for different types of positions could be crucial to your search, and ultimately a great timesaver for you. Résumé customization is crucial to reaching the top of the "must interview" stack as opposed to languishing in a pile with other second or third tier candidates. While a "one size fits all" résumé would be ideal in a perfect world, it is likely that the type of positions you may be applying for will vary – some may be more hands on, while others more management oriented, so you will need more than one style of résumé. For example, for positions not in your recent background, you may want a style that is written to showcase your capabilities, as opposed to emphasizing your more recent skill set. Don't be surprised if during your job search you end up with five or six versions of your résumé depending upon the types of positions you apply for.

Track which résumé you send to each employer so you know which version to have in front of you for phone interview, and of course which one to take with you to an in-person interview. You will want to take multiple copies of your résumé with you to each interview – one for you and one to give to each person that you meet with. The interviewer may have a copy of the résumé already, but if you have made updates to it, it is important they have the latest version on quality paper stock and not just plain white paper. You will make a positive impression on the interviewer that you planned ahead to make sure that they have a copy of your resume.

Keep an electronic copy of your cover letter and a copy of the job description, as these will be helpful when you have a phone and in-person interviews. Doing this will provide insight into the requirements and duties for the position, as well as let you know which version of the résumé and cover letter you sent them.

Use the spelling and grammar functions built into your word processing software to help you develop a well written résumé and cover letter. Import your résumé and cover letters into Google Translator to read your documents back to you. The audio feature will point out grammatical mistakes and allow you to hear how the résumé actually sounds aloud. Poor grammar, spelling errors, inconsistencies in tense, and formatting are some of the most common mistakes that people make on résumés. These mistakes show inattention to detail that potential employers will pick up on and compel them to move your résumé into the reject pile without having given it serious consideration. These mistakes can easily be avoided by using a spell checker and asking others to review the résumé. An additional set of eyes and a different perspective on what you have written is crucial and can provide insight you may not have considered otherwise.

Create your résumé on commonly used word processing software such as Microsoft Word or Adobe so that these files can easily be opened and imported into applicant tracking systems, as well as those involved in the hiring process.

Small, inappropriate, or difficult to read type fonts may not look professional or appropriate for your level or type of position and will look out of place when compared to other candidates applying for the same job. So, in addition to content, you will want to choose a font style and size that looks professional, is easy to read and makes the reader want to stay on the page instead of going on to the next résumé.

Avoid using headers, footers, borders, multiple columns, or "cells" of text on the résumé. These can sometimes cause conflicts with various applicant tracking systems that are used by employers to manage who has applied for various positions. You definitely don't want to have a résumé that gets bumped out of the system, nor do you want to create work for anyone who has to go in by hand to tweak your résumé.

Most people apply for jobs online due to the expediency and ease of forwarding résumés electronically, both for them and the employer. However, also sending résumés and cover letters via the postal service on professional looking stationery with matching envelopes will make your résumé stand out from the stack of résumés sitting on the recruiter or hiring manager's desk. Obviously, stationery and postage are an added expense and require time to prepare, but they are a nice touch that will make you stick out from the competition.

Similarly, creating your own personal business card that contains things such as the type of work that you do, key skills, degree, certifications, and contact information is something that you can easily carry with you and give to someone who may be able to help with your job search.

How long should a résumé be?

The general rule of thumb is that your résumé should cover the most recent 10-15 years of your work history or 2-3 pages, at most. Many recruiters prefer just one or two pages, but depending upon your experience, skillset and type of work that you do, three pages (at a maximum) will allow you to cover things that are relevant to your work history.

When should I update my résumé? What to include and what to leave out?

The short answer is you should update your résumé when you have "résumé worthy" items to add. As time goes on, it is easy to forget about projects or tasks that you have completed or were a part of. Frequently updating your résumé and online social media profiles such as LinkedIn, will ensure that you do not overlook key things that should be included on these things. You can always remove things in the future, but if you forget to add them, that option is null and void. That overlooked experience may have been something that would have been the extra nugget to make your résumé stick out from the hundreds of others that are sometimes reviewed for any given job opening.

Should I use a résumé service to help me put my résumé together?

Does your résumé force the reader's eye off the page or make them want to dig deeper? Does your résumé contain information that is relevant to the positions you are applying for? Are your writing skills below average, average, or top-notch? Are you able to concisely detail what you have done for each position that you have held? Can you compile that information into a format that not only illustrates your experience, but is also in a style that makes the recruiter want to spend more than the average of 6 seconds reviewing your résumé? If not, seeking the help of a professional could save you time and potentially help with landing a position much sooner than you might have otherwise.

Good Résumé Information

Recruiters use keyword searches when looking for résumés of potential candidates. It is imperative that your résumé contain terms common to your industry and illustrative of your experience. Information on the types of software you have experience with, products or services, employer names, degrees and certifications are all examples of things to include.

Recent college graduates may want to include their grade point average (GPA) if it is an impressive number. However, including a 2.0 GPA may not make the desired impression, so if your GPA is a high number, you may want to include it.

Things to Avoid

Pictures, flags, cartoons or graphic images are distracting and not appropriate to have on a résumé. Cartoonists, graphic designers, photographers and such should provide links to their online portfolios or provide attachments illustrating their work.

Email addresses should contain some variation of your full name. Using an email such as Skaterboyforlife@xyzmail.com is not appropriate for a Chief Financial Officer to use.

While famous quotes may reflect your personality, philosophy, or outlook on life, they have no relevance to your viability as a candidate and are taking up space that could be used to highlight your skills.

If you are deciding whether something seems questionable to include, it is probably better left off the résumé.

Important Tips

Your résumé should include your address, email address and at least one phone number. Your outgoing voicemail message should be professional, friendly-sounding, and clearly state your name. Having music, an excessively long, unusual, or annoying outbound voicemail message will raise unnecessary concerns in a potential employer.

There are multiple résumé styles; which is right for me?

There are multiple online resume building websites that can assist you in developing a resume, so explore those to provide insight on which style and format is best for you. There are two primary résumé styles – chronological and functional.

Chronological (Reverse Chronological)

Chronological or reverse chronological) is the typical style that most people choose. This style works well if you have a consistent work history that is relevant to your future employment goals. It easily can showcase your increasing levels of responsibility and duties.

On the flip side, this style may not be the right style for you if you have large gaps in employment, you change jobs frequently, or if you are transitioning to a new career.

Reverse chronological résumés list your most recent jobs at the top and work further back in time. Most hiring manager and recruiters prefer this style as it shows your most recent experience first, since older positions tend to carry less relevance than recent ones.

Functional Résumé

This style is commonly referred to as a "skills profile" as it allows you to focus more on your capabilities as opposed to focusing on things you did in specific positions. Those using this style like the fact that it allows you to showcase the skills you choose want to emphasize. While this style can be great to emphasize experience and accomplishments, it is often used to hide inconsistent work history, gaps in employment, or forays into other fields. Many employers tend to not like this style as it seems some people use this to emphasize their potential or capability as opposed to listing what they have actually done. Employers tend to find this style requires more guesswork about what a person has done and how current their skills may be. This uncertainty can make it difficult for hiring managers and recruiters to decide whether to pursue a candidate for an interview.

It should be noted that this style can be helpful if you are attempting to change careers and want to highlight recent training/education more so than relevant employment history.

Sample Résumé Format Sections and details to include

John Smith

123 Main Street, Washington, DC 20001

Home Phone (555) 555-5555 / Cell Phone (444) 444-4444

Email <u>JohnSmith@MyEmailAddress.com</u>

LinkedIn Profile Link

US citizen with current DOD Top Secret Clearance

OVERVIEW
Extensive experience with transactional replication, SQL mirroring and log shipping. Configured and managed many Active/Passive and Active/Active servers. Skilled with analyzing stored procedures and query performance using query execution plan, SQL profiler, Database Engine tuning advisor and performance monitor and is familiar with DMVs for monitoring activity.

EDUCATION

- Master's Degree in Computer Science, ABC University, Washington, DC
- Bachelor of Science in Computer Science, ABC University, Washington, DC

TRAINING/CERTIFICATIONS

- ITIL v3 Foundations
- Microsoft Certified Technology Specialist: SQL Server 2008, Implementation and Maintenance
- CompTIA Security+CE

CLEARANCE

- Department of Defense, Top Secret

WORK EXPERIENCE

ABC Products, Inc., March 2016 – Present

Senior Database Administrator

- Administer a mixed SQL environment of SQL 2012, 2014 and a few 2008 R2 servers. Installed and configured many SQL servers including configuring windows clustering and SQL high availability.
- Responsible for working closely with developers, project managers, management and engineering to facilitate successful implementation of projects.
- Created many SOP documentation for installing SQL, configuring SQL, High Availability and Windows clusters.
- Maintain over 50 SQL servers in a Development, Test, UAT and Pre-Production environment.

DEF Corporation, July 2014 – February 2015

Senior Database Administrator

- Administered mixed SQL server environment of SQL 2005, 2008 R2 and 2012 servers in a support contract with a federal agency.
- Responsible for monitoring and maintenance of all SQL database servers.
- Supported the SQL databases in a SharePoint 2010 farm.
- Provided backend support for custom applications, modifying and making additions as needed.

GHI Technology Inc., December 2011 – June 2014

Senior Database Administrator

- Administered mixed SQL server environment, SQL 2000, 2005, 2008 R2 on a federal contract.
- Supported a large SharePoint environment.
- Worked with engineering team to move from previous version of SharePoint/SQL to latest SharePoint and migration of SQL from 2005 to 2008 R2.
- All servers built as Active/Active clusters. Performed performance analysis and performance tracking.

JKL Systems, September 2003 – December 2011

Database Administrator

- Administered mixed SQL server environment in a contract with the Office of the President.
- Production Support Lead DBA in a 24x7 environment.

- Supported hundreds of databases, many being VLDBs. Replicated databases using transactional replication with independent distributors built on SQL clusters. Extensive work with replication, log shipping, database maintenance, indexing, backups, restores, DTS, BCP, script review, production implementations, SQL Compare and Visual Studio 2008 for schema and data comparisons, an auditing software, account creation, maintenance and other tasks in a mixed SQL 2000, 2005, 2008 R2 and 2012 environment.
- Set up partitioned tables using SQL 2005 partitioning and worked with BCVs in an EMC SAN.
- Was lead DBA, responsible for supervising the daily tasks of a staff of six DBAs.
- Was Cognos administrator, responsible for creating reports and troubleshooting query and performance issues.

<u>Special Awards and Recognition:</u>

Employee of the Month Awards: August 2007, April 2008, March 2013.

Received special bonus for recommending new technology and procedures that led to a large company contract award.

Chapter Two

Determining Who You Are

Self-Assessment and Satisfying the Inner You

To set yourself up for success in your next position, it is important that you do a self-assessment. What are you looking for in a new job or career? Will the jobs you are looking at fulfill you emotionally and financially? Will they motivate you to get up every day, endure the commute, and provide you with a sense of accomplishment? True self-reflection provides insight into strengths and weaknesses and goes a long way into preparation needed for a successful job search.

Why are you looking for a job? What is your motivation for looking for a new job? How do I find the right job for me?

In a perfect world, the ideal time to look for a job is when you already have one. It is less stressful to conduct a search when you have the security of a steady paycheck and are not pushed to just accept a position because you have a mortgage or car note hanging over your head. However, things such as unexpected layoffs, mergers, and a fluctuating economy can all prompt forced job changes with little to no warning.

If your current position is secure and you are looking for a job because you don't like the management style or the position does not pay enough to meet your expenses, maybe the issue doesn't lie with the position itself. Maybe it is time to look inward and figure out why you are unhappy and why you may be setting yourself up to repeat your current situation.

If you have met every challenge, produced record levels of revenue, successfully managed shrinking budgets with a stressed-out workforce that was asked to do more with fewer resources, then maybe it is time to take your skills and experience to a new environment.

If you were fired due to performance, then self-reflection and ownership of those mistakes are absolutely crucial in picking up the pieces and moving onward to the next position. Your challenges will be greater, but owning those mistakes or shortfalls will go a long way toward helping present yourself in a positive way. And, remember, taking ownership of mistakes and using them as a learning experience will help change your mind set about the situation and position you for future success. Many employers will appreciate your candidness when it comes to admitting you are human, versus blaming others for your situation. No one wants to hire someone who speaks negatively about a former employer or supervisor.

What positions are you targeting and why?

Every job hunter needs to know the type of job they want, but more importantly, what type of jobs they truly qualify for.

If the job you want is not one you are qualified for, figure out how you can meet the requirements - classes, internships, volunteering, or working with a mentor. Establish a clear and sustainable path to obtain that type of positon in the future.

For those who know what they want and have the requisite training and skills, the path is shorter, but will require a plan of attack. It has been said that looking for a job is a job itself, as it takes a lot of time and energy. If you are in a field with a lot competition for a limited number of openings in your area, what sets you apart from others – training, certifications, a degree, or a security clearance? Is the field one with growth and stability, or one with limited opportunities? Are the types of jobs you want geographically accessible to you? If not, are you willing to relocate or is it possible for you to work remotely?

If you know the type of position that you want, the next step is to find employers offering these positions.

Who do you want to work for and why? The internet can provide a wealth of information on potential employers. Using specific sites such as www.LinkedIn.com is a great resource to prospect for employers, find contacts at your targeted employers, find job postings and uncover information on leaders within your chosen field.

If you haven't already created a LinkedIn profile, do it now. Your résumé contains information that you should include. Look at profiles of people in your industry to see what others include on their profiles to help guide you. These profiles are a great way for recruiters and colleagues to find you or someone with your background. So, the more information and keywords it contains to help people to find you, the better.

Chapter Three

First impressions

Look in the Mirror

Take an honest look at yourself in the mirror. Do you make a good first impression? How would you appear to a potential employer? Do you dress professionally or appropriately for the position you have or aspire to? Do you appear "up-to-date" and confident? If not, what changes can you make to feel and look that way?

Being aware of potential employer concerns allows you to make a more conscious decision about your appearance choices and help you to make a great first impression.

Is your hair neatly cut and currently in style, or does it look the same as it did 10 or 20 years ago? Is it potentially distracting to an interviewer or would it be considered dangerous in performing the job you want? Are you in need of a new cut, style, or dye job? If so, don't wait until the day before your interview to take action. What if something happens that prevents you from going as expected, or you end up with a bad cut or color? Knowing that you look the part will help with building confidence.

Do you wear jewelry? Is it distracting or more suited for a nightclub than a professional environment? Too much jewelry, especially the kind that clangs, reflects light, and looks unprofessional, can be distracting in an interview. Facial jewelry, piercings, and exposed tattoos can leave a negative impression on some hiring managers, especially for those where the position would require customer interaction.

Do you wear makeup, perfume, or cologne? Less is usually more when it comes to these things. Overpowering smells, especially in an enclosed office, make breathing difficult or uncomfortable for those sensitive to strong scents.

Make sure that your shoes are neatly polished and not dirty or scuffed. Shoes should be comfortable and not too high as to be unstable or dangerous if you have to tour a manufacturing facility or go up and down lots of stairs.

If you have belt loops on your pants or slacks, then you need to wear a belt.

Whatever clothing you wear, you need to feel comfortable and confident in it. Make sure your outfit is not too tight or too baggy. Just as important, make sure it is freshly laundered or dry cleaned, and not wrinkled or stained. If you have a limited wardrobe or clothing budget, check out local thrift stores such as Goodwill for something suitable. Many cities also have organizations that will provide those in need with appropriate attire.

If wearing a suit, make sure that your suit, shirt (or blouse), and tie match appropriately. Belts and shoes should be the same color. There are many books and magazines devoted to proper attire, so be sure to check some out if you feel you could use some additional help with your clothing choices.

Chapter Four

Social Media: Friend or Enemy? Both!

Social Media –The Good, the Bad, and the Insanely Stupid

Most people have some sort of social media profile such as LinkedIn, Facebook, or Twitter. What you may not be aware of is that many hiring managers and company human resource professionals check social media profiles, whether they have an official policy or not.

There are companies that are paid to scour the internet looking at social media profiles and "questionable content"? Is there anything you posted that you regret? Do you really want a future boss or co-worker to see your vacation pictures, holding bottles of tequila when you were underage, or rappelling off the side of the football stadium? In the United States, everyone has the right to express their opinions on various topics without fear of persecution, but it can impact hiring. Will posting that diatribe, bad joke or political statement make a difference in the world if you express it online? Do you have pictures or posts online that would be better not being seen by anyone outside your immediate circle of friends? A general rule of thumb that may help you to think before you post would be – if your grandmother, pastor, or your future self were to view the post, would there be disappointment or embarrassment? Would you likely wish it had never been posted? If so, get rid of those posts now, un-tag yourself and ask friends to think before they post and tag you by name.

The bottom line is you never know if someone who has the ability to hire you (or not), will look at these things and call into question your ability to represent their organization.

Network, Network, Network – Always Be Networking

Many jobs are filled before they are ever posted. How can that be? The short answer is that many jobs are filled by people that were referred to the company by peers or former supervisors. Maintaining your network of contacts is crucial to you and those in your network. Technology makes it easier to maintain contact and reach out to others. Don't be shy in letting others know you are open to new job opportunities even when you are not actively looking. On the flip side, you should be willing to help others in the job market and serve as a reference for them, if possible. Helping someone find a great job is rewarding and can create bonds that can last a lifetime.

Chapter Five

The Why's and the How's of Job Hunting

Are you comfortable being a salaried employee, hourly contractor, or 1099 employee? Knowing the differences and understanding your level of comfort with each type can either open you up to other opportunities or narrow the number of positions you apply for. Keeping your options open will provide more opportunities for you to choose from.

Goal Setting

You should set daily or weekly goals to devote a certain amount of time looking for new positions. A serious approach to your job search will help you maintain momentum and maximize your opportunities. If you treat the search as a part or fulltime job, you will see greater success in your search. A half-hearted approach in your effort will lead to frustration, and the time you did devote will likely have been wasted.

Organizational Tips

Having multiple versions of your of résumé specific for the types of jobs you are targeting will make applying for jobs faster and more efficient for you.

Create a spreadsheet and copy the online job descriptions into it including the company name, position title, description, company URL (i.e., www.abccompany.com), specific job application URLs if applicable, and any names and phone numbers of people that you come in contact with at the organization. Having this information organized and accessible should make follow-up easy. Make note of which version of your résumé you submitted. You should absolutely review this information prior to telephone and in-person interviews.

Job Boards

Many industries have some job boards specific to positions typically found in their industry, so be sure to post your résumé and look for jobs on those websites. You should also post your résumé on other job boards such as the ones listed below. Having your résumé on multiple job boards opens you up to more potential job opportunities and offers. Below are a few popular websites that allow you to post résumés, search open positions and set up search agents:

-www.Monster.com

-www.Indeed.com

-www.CareerBuilder.com

-www.Local.com

-www.LinkedIn.com

-www.Dice.com

-www.TheLadders.com

-www.Job.com

-www.Craigslist.com

-www.Net-Temps.com

Companies normally have to pay fees to access résumés and candidate contact information. However, with websites like Craigslist that are accessible and free for anyone to use, for safety reasons, you may not want to include your street address on the resume that you post on there. If you enter "jobs" into a search engine such as Google, you'll see how many job boards there actually are. Choose the ones whose names you recognize as a starting point. Don't overlook the local classified newspapers, as they are still a place where companies will advertise jobs. If your industry has trade associations, it is quite possible they may have job postings available to members, so look at those websites as well. Joining those associations may be helpful not only for finding jobs, but also staying current on the industry. The membership may be something to include on your résumé. And, as an added bonus, the membership may be tax deductible.

Utilize social media websites such as LinkedIn and Facebook to let others know you are open to job opportunities. These sites can also be searched for job opportunities.

Many job boards will allow you to create "Search Agents" that alert you to new job openings and will email new positions to you daily as they are posted. Websites such as www.Local.com www.SimplyHired.com and www.Indeed.com consolidate open positions from multiple resources and may have some duplicates. However, there is a strong likelihood that not all local positions will be on each job board, so it is recommended that you utilize multiple job boards for searching, setting up search agents, and for posting your résumé online.

When searching for positions, keep in mind that within some fields, many terms can mean the same thing and are used interchangeably. You will want to use multiple terms when setting up search agents and when searching for positions.

Update your résumé every few days on the job boards. Updating can be something as simple as logging in and adding a period or asterisk and then removing it so the system recognizes that a change has been made. Doing this innocuous exercise will make your résumé appear as though it was updated, even if you are not making any significant changes. This will keep your résumé near the top of recruiter's search results as opposed to being buried several pages deep because your résumé has not been updated for weeks or months.

Cover Letters

While cover letters are sometimes read by hiring manager, oftentimes they are not. It is generally accepted that a candidate will be perceived as more professional if they include a well-written cover letter that is tailored to the position for which they are applying. Creating cover letters requires some extra work, which is why many people skip this step. Just like having multiple résumés tailored to various types of positions, having multiple cover letter templates will help you to speed up the application process and position you to be taken seriously as a candidate.

Staffing Agencies and Executive Search firms

Making contact with staffing agencies and executive search firms can open up a multitude of opportunities that are not advertised by employers directly. Organizations will use these outside companies if they are having a difficult time finding suitable candidates; they do not have adequate time, staff or resources to recruit for the role; they may not want to be directly involved in the process; or may not want to let competitors or employees know they are looking to hire for certain positions.

Most staffing agencies and executive search firms will have areas that they specialize in, so focus on the ones that will likely have the types of roles you are seeking.

"Shotgun" or "Sniper" Approach

Most people use keyword searches when looking for jobs online. Some will use very specific keywords to narrow the search to exactly the types of positions they are searching for. This approach is typically used by those that know what they want and go about targeting and applying for only those positions that meet their strict criteria. These folks tend to have the "sniper" mentality and don't want to waste their "bullets" or time applying for positions that are not within the confines of their desired roles. These people usually tend to be further along in their careers and have specific skill sets.

Others will take a more broad approach with the "shotgun" method and apply for positions well above, below, or outside their skillset and capability level. Why do they do this? Quite possibly, they are looking for a job, any job, and not a career; they are open to trying new things, are just entering the workforce for the first time, or reentering after a hiatus. Some people approach it as a fishing expedition hoping to land something, really anything, without really making a plan.

Recruiters tend to frown upon those applying for jobs for which they are not even remotely qualified. It is viewed as a waste of the candidate's time, the recruiter's time, and the company's resources to review unqualified résumés. If your background doesn't remotely match the requirements for a particular position, move onto the next opening that is likely to lead somewhere.

Do Your Research

Before you apply for any job or go to an interview you need to know something about the company you are applying to, especially if you are crafting a customized and detailed cover letter that explains your candidacy for the position. Google the company name and see what comes up; look at their website, check out online resources such as Hoovers, Glassdoor, Twitter, LinkedIn, and Facebook to get a sense of their corporate structure, leadership, and how they present themselves. Read customer reviews to see what others think. Have they won any contracts or industry awards? Have they had lawsuits against them? Would you likely be comfortable in an organization of their size? Do you know anyone that is a current or former employee?

Do you have an interview scheduled? Google the names of the people you will be meeting with. Check out their LinkedIn, Facebook, and Twitter accounts. Do they list any hobbies or interests that you may have in common? How long have they been with the company? Who do they report to? What is the tone of their posts? Do they seem friendly, serious, or likeable? Being able to glean some information from these profiles may help identify common interests, give you some insight into their personality and provide you with potential topics to discuss during an interview.

Applicant Tracking Systems and the Black Hole

Most companies use some sort of Applicant Tracking System to manage résumés, post jobs to their careers page and social media websites, and help to meet federal equal employment opportunity laws. You will be required to completely fill out the application and provide truthful information covering a range of topics.

A job application is considered a legal document and you will be required to sign and acknowledge that the information is correct and true. Providing misinformation such as adding an extra year onto a job that you held, stating that you completed a degree when you have not, or providing anything that is not accurate, will be considered dishonest and employers will remove you from consideration. Should the misinformation not be caught immediately, it can be grounds for dismissal or legal action if found at out some point in the future.

Applications can vary, but most will request your full legal name (maiden name if applicable); social security number; address; prior address; type of position you are seeking; full-time or part-time preference; current and prior employer information including address, phone number, supervisor name and contact information; education information such as schools and colleges attended, trade schools; military service; any criminal history and more. You will likely be asked for permission for the company run a background check on you as a condition of employment.

References

Having a list of supervisory references along with their contact information is crucial. You will need to provide this as part of the application process. The hiring manager or human resources department will likely request it, too. Most employers will ask to contact former supervisors (or current manager, if possible). Not being able to provide adequate references sends up red flags to someone for hiring managers. It is wise to ask former supervisors to serve as a reference for you ahead of time so they do not receive an unexpected call and are caught off-guard. Not only will this let them know you are in the market for a position, it will give you a sense of their willingness to help in your search and how good of a reference they will provide. Be sure to let them know there is a possibility they may receive calls from more than one person or company. They are doing you a favor by offering to serve as a reference, so make them aware that you appreciate the time and energy they put forth on your behalf. Once you have accepted a new position, be sure to reach out to them and share your good news. You should also send them a handwritten "thank you" note. A small token of your appreciation is also a nice gesture.

Chapter Six

The Interview, Preparation Tips, Research, Questions to Ask, and More...

Practice Interviewing and Perfecting Your Pitch

The best way to make the interview process more comfortable is to make sure you are prepared for the interview and can confidently handle questions you might be asked. Ask a friend to sit down and subject you to the "hot seat" by asking questions you would expect to be asked in an interview. Make them go deeper with follow up questions and not just accept cursory answers from you. Going through this process will help you to feel confident and comfortable when it comes time for a real interview.

Use these practice sessions as opportunities to learn how to turn tough questions into good conversational talking points about why you are a good fit for the position. Really good interviews are more conversational in nature than a question and answer session, so work on developing ways to build rapport with the interviewer. This will help put both you and the interviewer at ease. Be sure to ask questions that provide insight into the position while also creating opportunities to illustrate your experience and capability to meet their needs. Asking the interviewer things such as how long they have been employed there and why they have stayed can provide real insight into the company while also taking an interest in them personally. These are also great conversation starters.

Everyone should have a 30-second elevator pitch about why they would make a great employee and how they can make an impact for the organization. Using the job description as a guideline to draw from can help you to highlight your skills and differentiators. Create a few short "sound bites" that you can use throughout the interview to sell yourself and as a closing point when wrapping up the interview.

In-person Interviews

You should expect the interview to start as soon as you enter the property grounds. The guard at the front gate, the receptionist, or the person you encounter on the elevator may pass along their observations to the interviewer. They may be the interviewer or owner's brother, wife or third cousin. Some companies will ask everyone that encountered the interviewee about their impression of the person – were they friendly and professional, or seemed rushed and rude?

You should arrive approximately 10 minutes, but no more than 15 minutes, before the scheduled interview time. Be sure to be courteous, friendly, and observant of the surroundings. Make a mental note of the people walking through the office or facility, and the mood of those you see. Do they look happy or stressed? Is there background music, and if so, what type? It may give you some insight into the environment. Browse through company magazines or marketing collateral or reports that may be sitting out for visitors, and ask if you can have a copy. What is the dress code of those that you see – is it professional, business casual? These are all things that provide insight into the company, and are potential topics of discussion.

Be You

Research shows that over 50% of recruiters factor a candidate's personality into whether they could be a good fit for the company's environment. Nearly 50% of recruiters view how well a candidate presents themselves in interviews as a big differentiator in whether or not they move forward to the next step in the interviewing process.

While it is important to put on your "game face" and be professional, confident, and friendly during the interview process, it is imperative that you also be yourself and exhibit some of your personality, so both you and the interviewer know whether the position is a good fit for you and the employer. Companies hire people to perform tasks, and while these people have skills, they also have attributes, quirks, and personality traits that can be crucial to success or failure. In interviews many people put up walls or exhibit fake personalities due to nervousness. It is important that you relax and allow your true self to shine during the interview. Those who put up a façade ultimately are doing themselves and their potential employer a disservice.

When a bad hiring situation occurs it can lead to frustration on everyone's part, but the fault ultimately lies with the candidate. Repeated cycles of this occurring or blaming the employer for a job "not working out" could be avoided by being yourself, doing the self-assessment mentioned in Chapter 2 and knowing your likes and dislikes. Taking the time to do the assessment will save you and others from wasting time, energy, resources and avoid potentially bad situations. So, for better (or worse), let your true personality shine a bit when interviewing. It will be the best thing you do and allow you to find a long-term position in an environment that suits you.

The Handshake

Always extend your hand first and introduce yourself saying your first and last name. Smile and make eye contact as you shake hands. A firm grip is always desired both as a giver and a receiver, and is interpreted normally as a sign of confidence. One recent study concluded that applicants with firm handshakes received stronger "hire" recommendations than those who provided less firm handshakes.

There is psychology behind various handshake styles. The most common is the single hand shake and is viewed as friendly and professional. A single hand shake where one person extends their hand with their palm down and the other person with their palm up can signify dominance and submissiveness. Using two hands like in a regular handshake, but with the person using their left hand to also grip the person's hand is usually a sign of affection or enthusiasm for the other person.

You should take precaution to make sure you do not offer weak, sweaty or cold grips. If your hands are typically moist or get that way when nervous, discretely wipe your hand before extending it.

Demeanor

Sell yourself – be confident and personable, but not cocky; be someone a hiring manager would want to invite to dinner.

People instinctively feel a connection to those that are like themselves. Mirroring the interviewer's enthusiasm, body language, and pace of speaking will subconsciously help build rapport. Doing these things can create a sense of trust, comfort, and familiarity when someone looks or sounds like us.

Be sure to use good posture by standing and sitting up straight. When sitting, keep your feet close together. Do not place anything on the interviewer's desk or invade their personal space in any way.

Oversharing

While the interview process is designed to determine a person's ability to do a job, be sure that you do not give out too much information. Make sure you answer their questions fully, but also ensure you don't talk too much or off topic.

While you want to build rapport and get to know the interviewer, you must be careful to not overshare personal information that may take you out of the running for the job. Talking about how the police were called to the party you attended last weekend, or how you have a hard time getting up on Fridays as you typically go bar hopping on Thursdays, will not leave the interviewer with a positive impression. Even though you may feel you are bonding with the interviewer, bear in mind they are evaluating you every second that you are in their office, and are making judgements about your ability to do the job, and how you will represent their organization.

Questions – What to ask, What not to ask

Preparing yourself for the interview starts with researching the organization. You need to understand what they do, what differentiates them from similar organizations, and figure out how you can fit in. Finding out what they do beyond just what is involved with your potential position is crucial. Taking an interest and demonstrating enthusiasm and understanding of what they do will set you apart from the average applicant.

Ask questions that show you have done your homework on them that is relevant to your area of expertise.

You need to understand the position description and know it inside and out. Be prepared to talk about details and expectations and what you can bring to the table to help meet their objectives.

When answering questions, pause to think over the answer for a moment. If you are unsure of what they are asking, ask them to repeat the question to make sure you provide them with the information they are seeking.

Some interviewers are like professional poker players. They never show their hand and hope to make you sweat to see how you respond. This may or may not be how they operate on a daily basis, but could be an indication of their management style.

Many people involved in the interview process are not comfortable with that task or may not be sure what they can ask. They may hire only a few people per year, if that, and may not be competent interviewers. If you sense that may be the case, help put them at ease by asking them questions about the company, how long they have been there, what they like about their role. This can create a great opportunity to build rapport, sell yourself as a good fit for the position, and gain insight that you may not have gotten otherwise.

Often, hiring managers rush through the interview if they feel you are not qualified or seem unsure of your abilities, or if you illustrate a lack of depth in your answers. So, if you sense they are not comfortable with your response, provide additional examples that show your level of competency so they understand that you could be a valuable team member. You want them to feel that they received the information they were looking for and with a high level of satisfaction in the way you delivered it.

Some interviewers will go through your résumé position by position, so be sure that you know it inside and out. You should be able to recall skills and other specifics encountered at each position, along with the dates of employment. Many people inadvertently trip themselves up by not spending time to reflect on things they have done in the past and thinking about how those things could translate into the position they are interviewing for.

Be prepared to explain challenges you have encountered, what you did to overcome those challenges, what you learned about the process, and what you might do differently having had the benefit of hindsight.

Inquiring about what a position pays in the initial interview is frowned upon and will leave a negative impression of your social and professional graces. The employer will interpret that as you not understanding generally accepted protocol. During the initial interview, the employer will not have had adequate time to reflect on the interview, your capabilities, and what they may be able to pay for someone with your experience and potential. Give yourself an opportunity to work through the interview process and let them see your worth. There will be time for salary discussions at the appropriate time.

What to Take to the Interview

Carrying a nice leather portfolio binder with a pad and pen to take notes makes you look prepared and professional. You will want to make a few notes either during or shortly after the interview of key things you gleaned from the interview or things you need to do as a follow up to the meeting.

While great in theory to have a list of questions in your head, it is important to have a short list of topics or questions written down at your fingertips that you can glance at to make sure that you cover everything that is important to you. You can also refer to these to help avoid lulls in the conversation.

Group Interviews

Many companies like to conduct group interviews. So don't be surprised if you sit down with more than one person during your interview. Be sure to say hello, shake hands, and introduce yourself to everyone. It is important that you make eye contact with each individual throughout the interview.

Post Interview/Follow up Tips – Notes, Emails, and Phone Calls

Be sure to obtain the business card of everyone that you interview with so you have the correct spelling of their name, title, and email address so you can follow up with future questions and expressions of continued interest. While sending an email is the fastest way to communicate with the interviewer and allows you to have an open line of communication, the best way to stand out from other candidates is to send a follow-up letter through the mail on nice stationery. Most people tend to overlook doing this and solely rely on email as the method to follow-up. A written card or typed letter sent through mail thanking them for their time will leave an impression, and should be done in conjunction with an email.

How Much Contact is Too Much? When to Let Go and Cut Your Losses?

It is important that you show your continued interest in the position and desire to schedule another interview if that is the next step in the process. Frequent calls, voicemails or too many emails will turn off just about any hiring manager. They may sense that you are desperate for a job, difficult to work with, or even feel that you are stalking them. An email as a follow-up to an interview is absolutely fine. However, showing up at their kid's soccer game is not a good idea. Put yourself in their shoes and imagine how you would feel if the situation were reversed and you received numerous phone calls or emails on a weekly basis from the same person. You would likely tend to view them unfavorably and remove them from consideration.

Just because you had a great interview does not mean you will receive an offer. It is important that you continue your search until you have an offer for the job that you want. After leaving multiple voicemails or having emails go unanswered, it is probably a sign to move on. While the hiring manager may have had good intentions by telling you that you looked like a great fit, someone else may have been an even better fit for the role. If they have not reached out to you in some way to explain that they have had an unexpected delay in the process or why things are taking longer than anticipated, what they are not saying may be the most telling sign of all. Never assume that an offer is coming until you have it in hand. Move on to the next prospective job and don't let their delay or lack of communication slow your momentum in continuing to interview elsewhere.

What if you are not offered a position?

Many companies will let you know that an offer has been extended or that a position has been filled. It is unfortunate, but many will never follow-up in any way to communicate the news.

If you feel you were an extremely strong candidate and were a finalist for the role, you may want to reach out to the hiring manager through an email expressing your disappointment in not receiving the offer, but again, thanking them for their time. This is another opportunity for you to show your professionalism, build additional rapport, and ask them to keep you in mind for future positions. This would also be the time to inquire about a quick meeting or phone call to ask for feedback on any areas where you came up short in their eyes. Any feedback they offer could be crucial in helping you in future interviews, there or elsewhere.

Chapter Seven

I received an offer, now what?

Compensation and Negotiating

What do positions you are interviewing for typically pay for someone with your level of experience? You can't really negotiate salary or an hourly rate if you don't know this information. There are multiple sources of reliable salary information on websites like Glassdoor (www.glassdoor.com) and Career Builder (www.careerbuilder.com) to name a few.

Benefits such as healthcare insurance are important for most people. Will the company pay for benefits or at least a portion? What about vacation and other paid time off such as sick days or holidays? What type of retirement plan do they have? Do they offer a matching contribution? Many companies have set policies on not providing extra paid time off or paying for things such as car and cell phone allowance, tuition and certification reimbursement, or a gym membership. But, many companies will negotiate these types of things into a compensation package in some cases. Be creative, confident and prepared when negotiating. If your salary requirement exceeds the maximum salary for the position, try asking for perks such as extra time off or the ability to telecommute occasionally. These types of things can be a huge factor and can lead to a higher quality of life and potentially better job performance.

The compensation package is important, but don't assume the first offer is the final offer if it is not meeting market conditions for your area, your experience level, or your expectation. If you do plan to negotiate, having cold, hard facts from a reliable source is crucial. Telling an employer that your cousin says you should be making X will not give you the credibility and bargaining power you are trying to establish. Having quantifiable research that you can share may give you the bargaining power you want. But, you should be prepared that the employer may not be able to offer more.

It is not uncommon for an organization to offer 10-25% over what you are currently earning, assuming you have a solid background, a skill set that is highly technical or in-demand, or special knowledge or certifications that are difficult to find.

As mentioned above, salary is just part of the overall package. If you are only looking at the salary portion of the package, you are missing the bigger picture. If you are focused solely on the salary and not focusing on how much you would enjoy the work and the environment, this may not be the position for you.

Companies that consistently underpay their employees tend to have higher turnover rates and many current and former disgruntled employees. Avoid these companies like the plague unless there is a legitimate reason for you to accept an offer such as skill-specific training, close proximity to home, or an opportunity to get experience in the industry. Otherwise, it is likely best to keep looking.

Accepting any position with the intent to continue job searching is morally and ethically wrong, and will reflect poorly on you, no matter your personal situation. Companies expend a tremendous amount of resources and manpower to get a candidate to the offer stage. You should be respectful and cognizant of that fact.

If you decline an offer, it should be done professionally, gracefully, and with tact. Keep in mind that you are rejecting someone who thought enough of you to offer you a job. Being anything less than gracious is uncalled for. Declining the offer professionally could establish dialogue for additional negotiation or a potential offer in the future. The same hiring manager you decline today could consider you in the future, or even at a different company, if you handle the situation with class and dignity.

Counter Offers

Unless there are really unusual circumstances (you are offered company equity, additional benefits and/or pay), you should never accept a counter offer to stay in your current position. If a company is not offering you more money, responsibility, vacation time, or whatever they decide to offer up before you started interviewing elsewhere, where did this windfall suddenly come from? They obviously had the ability to pay you more before, give you more responsibility, vacation time or more. Why they chose not to do it is the question and possibly part of the underlying reason you were looking to leave in the first place. Was your boss unknowing or uncaring regarding your level of dissatisfaction, and if so, why? Research shows that people who accept counteroffers usually end up leaving within 12 months anyway. Oftentimes, managers tend to look at these "retained employees" as disloyal and not being a team player. The residual carryover of these and other factors can make the work environment uncomfortable for the employee, their peers, and their supervisor. Will the extra money that you had to fight for really be worth it when the odds are that you are going to leave anyway, and your search will begin again?

In Conclusion

The job search can be a long and confusing process filled with obstacles you can't always foresee. Hopefully, this book has enlightened you as to how organizations handle the hiring process and has provided fresh insight and steps that will lead you to a more rewarding position in the next step in your career.